firstborn

Sarah Aluko

ISBN: 099572380X
ISBN-13:978-0995723801

Illustrated by Lola Betiku
Edited by Joy Odochi Mbakwe

For every season there is a poem.

CONTENTS

This is my child. I gave birth to her through some of the longest nights of my life. I owe her so much, for she healed me. She gave me honey when I became accustom to vinegar, brought purpose to my pain. She is so special to me because every time I looked into her eyes I saw myself. I saw who I wanted to be. She loved me out of my comfort zone. I had to remind myself that I was worthy of her, that she was good enough, that she deserved a chance to come into this world. I love her because she is unique. She does not have to compete with her brothers and sisters because there is no hierarchy only differences, and differences are beautiful.

So please be gentle with her. She's my firstborn.

To the reader, our new friend.

Dedicated to the ones I love.

DUSK

That time when the sun
is setting on our love
and all I can think about is
finding my way back to you.
When everything looks and
feels a little softer in the sunset.

DUSK

I was his favourite book
Hungry for each page
He said I was so easy to read
As he carefully unearthed a new chapter
With such compassion
He would use his fingers to
Highlight the parts that moved him
And his tongue to recite my words back to me
Thirsty
As if my words were water
He took his time to lap up every detail
He read in between my lines
All the things I could not say
Endless magical endings
I opened up every night.

What is the secret to your heart he asked?
I whispered back.
Consistency.

-        *Key*

Speak to me in kisses
It's the only language
I can understand right now.

The sweet sound of a Monday afternoon
As the sun sets on our union
Her warmth smiles at our love
Soft rays travel across
Our intertwined bodies
(local) birds sing our approval
As our spirits dance together in passion
Enjoying each other
Fatigue has swallowed our tongues
Words are not needed for this moment
Just his warm embrace
As he plays with the ends of my hair
Gently kisses my collar bone
Before he drifts off back to me
Physically dead to the world
I watch the face of beauty
Kiss his seductive lips
And join him back
in our dreams.

-    *Perfection*

Every smile always starts and ends with your name.

Your words always had a way of undressing me,
softly.
Until I am naked and ready
for whatever
you
have
to
give.

4 eyes
2 hearts
1 face
I think we're kissing…

Sometimes we just have to listen hard enough…

'I waited up for you…'
'Saved you a plate…'
'Be careful tonight'
'Of course I'll go with you…'
'Here, let me get that…'
'I'll drive…'

\-   *How he says I love you*

I love him like a best friend
Yet he kisses me like a husband
And I respond as his wife
He embraces me like a father
And I accept it as a loving daughter
He defends me as if he were my brother
And I support him like a sister
For no soul could ever understand.
Our simple but complicated,
Strangely fantastic,
Forever-loving, forever-changing, forever-growing
For mere mortals could never comprehend it.
So as he lies next to me
Smooth ebony skin to match mine
Pure strength. Defined by experience.
As if he were a reincarnation of
thousands of untold stories
Like the men who once birthed
the pyramids from the scars on their backs.
I stare into his eyes, as he holds me in his love.
I see the stars.
And continue to love him
Like a best friend.

This love is deep
Intense
I feel the weight of your love
holding me
Shortening breathes
Immense pleasure
Purifying pain
Until there is no more
An explosion of our insides merging
You know my secrets.
I am open
You come in
This feels like home.

-    *You- part (i)*

When I look at you
You remind me of a diamond
Covered in dirt. Rough edges.
Full of potential. Refined by pressure.
So close.
That through the fire I thought I was burning,
Still yearning
To get a sneak peak
Wondering if you would make it
But you came out brilliant
So forgive me if I stare too long.

-   *You- part (ii)*

Love is you.
A constant reminder that
God has not forgotten me
And this poem may not necessarily rhyme
Because you'll see in time
How much flowery words
and decorated verbs
Aren't enough to express
how much I love you.
Sometimes love cannot be
Contained in a poem
Explained in a poem
Sometimes similes and metaphors
are not enough
Sometimes love is awkward
Sometimes it doesn't communicate properly
Sometimes love wants to run away
as far as the oceans
Sometimes love has to find a middle ground
Sometimes love wonders if you are worth it
Sometimes.

-   *You- part (iii)*

I vow...
To keep your secrets. To support you.
To bring out the best in you. To encourage you.
Always give you a home in my heart.
To keep you comfortable.
That when the rest of the world is not on your side,
I will be.
To make it my mission that a smile is never far from your face. To
love you.
To listen, and not to listen with the intent to reply but just to listen.
To keep you safe.
To always be your friend. To put in effort.
To try.
All of this till the day I die
You see I forgot this was still a poem
And without rhyming words this may seem a tad dry
But I vow to open up inside
And I know you have to ask me like 15 times before
my response is more than *I'm fine*, but I vow that
will lessen in time
I vow to never mislead you.
I vow to always encourage you to stay on
the path that's right
I vow that these will be more than nouns but verbs
And even then,
this will be more than just mere words...

You- part (iv)

Lay me down in forever
and press pause on our moment.

Please can we get back to our song.

- *Missing you at 3 am*

There are times when you remind me of poetry
You appeal to the deepest parts of me
I stay up most nights wondering how you do it.

Your lips taste like forever.

I once made love to a man named knowledge
Who had his way with my mind
and played with my conscious
That night
I would meet his philosophical tongue,
as Pythagoras theorem lingers around my neck.
My arrogant soul wants to be on top.
Show him what I know.
My ignorant tongue fights back.
But his accomplished hands wrestle me into
submission, surrendering my womanhood.
Assimilating a damp enlightenment.
Taking in every inch of sophistication
So deep.
I can feel Picasso painting abdominal
masterpieces.
Relentlessly recreating a reincarnation
of beautiful memories.
Teaching me. Life cycles
Taking me to new limits
Unknown and beyond
The customary design of mental stimulation
My eyes find an unidentified brilliance
at the rear of my dome.

- *Tales of a Sapiosexual*

TWILIGHT

TWILIGHT

That time between darkness and sunrise
When the approaching blackness becomes your friend
My easy listener
She has swallowed all judgments into her abyss
She cannot see my tears
I can finally break into a million pieces
She does not expect me to be whole
The only place where I can be myself
Laying in her darkness. Vulnerable.
Ogling the moon, envying its wholeness. Together.

Mother says some men are bandits
Coming to take what they have not earned
She says bandits make temples out of bodies
Worshiping all night long, on their knees
Singing sweet songs of devotion
That are always forgotten by morning
Mother says they do not need bricks or mortar
Just blood and water
Because bandits live in bodies

Bandits live in my body.
Sat in my kitchen, eaten my food.
Some didn't mind the plate it was served on,
others too polite to say.
Bandits.
With their dirty feet on my kitchen table,
as if it was easy to clean up.
Full and fat. Fat men. Fat women.
All with opinions.
Tired.
They need a place to sleep,
some make it to the bedroom.
Most ask.
One didn't.
Selfish bastard. No home training.
I was thirteen.
I didn't know I needed locks.

Bandits live in my body.
Told me that I should lay my bed,
pick better sheets,
that my pillows are too soft, too big,
how could they ever leave?
Bursting at the seams. There is no room.
Mirrors have no function as I can hardly see myself.
Bursting at the seams. It's getting tight.
Buttons popping. This skirt is too fitted.
So now I can't walk, I sashay.
Being careful not to let the bandits out.
Before they call out to their friends,
hey there's room for one more.

Bandits live in my body.
At night they burrow holes in my heart.
Now sweet words only go straight through me.
I scream. *No, stop!*
Too beautiful for him to listen.
Crafty crooks, they traded my voice for aesthetics.
Collapsed lungs. No sound. But what is a voice if there is
no one in the house to hear it.

Bandits live in my body.
Started a revolt with my brain. Threatened a strike.
Said that they will leave me, afraid of being empty.

Bandits live in my body. Now I'm part of the furniture.
They say home is where the heart is but bandits have made
a home where my heart is.
So tell me where do I stay. Stranger in my own house.
Even my hands feel foreign so I can't reach out to save
myself.

Bandits live in my body.
I guess my mother did warn me that empty houses,
make cosy homes for lonely bandits.

-   *Bandits*

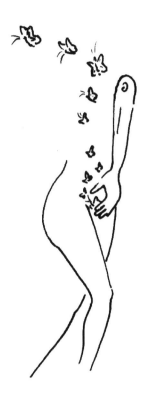

If he only comes
for the warmth
between your thighs
He does not love you.
Love does not ask you
to give something
for nothing.

I wonder if he remembers my face
Does he know it came with a name?
Can he still feel his unsatisfied hands pressed down on my neck?
Is that how bad he wanted my head?
Was I enough to stain the walls of his memory?
Did he know manipulation is a wonderful trap?
If I can't please you, then you need to please me
Finally, my first kiss. Big fat rubber lips.
Initially, resisting,
but still grabbing my hips.
Squirming around. Why are his hands so strong?
Is cupping my breasts meant to feel wrong?
Oh sweet, naïve lamb did you have to be slaughtered?
All I wanted was a kiss
Why didn't your tongue taste like fairytales and puppy love?
All I wanted was a kiss
Why didn't your tongue taste like the old sermons preached on
year 9 playgrounds?
All I wanted was a kiss. Who lied?
I was thirteen and he wasn't
If only I knew that day
We would exchange more than numbers
It would have been
Easier to just give me
bleach and a switchblade.
I mean there are so many more
pleasant ways to die.

-   *My hitman*

Tired.
Of men.
Who want to pick
My flowers.
But
Do not want the job of
Watering
The roots.

-   *Cowards*

The
Next time
You want something
To walk all over
Use a doormat.
Not my heart.

The heart, well,
She can be greedy
Consuming anything close enough
Anything or everything
Even she can't tell the difference
But can one blame her?
She needs love to thrive
But will settle for attention
just to survive.

- *Queen of Hearts*

Dear Independent Woman

You are perfect the way that you are
Don't let them lie to you
They'll tell you they love you
Don't be scared, they've got you
I'll hang up your cape, it's not you
Strip the 'S' off your chest, undress you
Climb into your heart, caress you
Morphine to the brain, they've stopped you
It was so easy to love you
Curiosity is gone they don't need you
Bleeding out, *I can't keep you*
This commitment you want *I can't please you*
Defences down, what's left of the real you?
You need him now; his words have weakened you
Left on the street corner, who's going to protect you?
Cardiac arrest, can his hands save you?
CPR needed, who's going to touch you?
Unintentionally abandoned, they think he's ruined you
But there's strength left to salvage the rest of you
Survivor. You've worked hard to become you
So guard the heart inside of you
Hold onto everything that is dear to you
Don't be quick to give them you
Wait for the one that deserves you
Through actions you can trust that he'll take care of you
Who can offer more than... I love you.

- *Monday morning's battle cry*

I am a rock.
In the heat of the sun
or at the punch of the tide.
I remain.
Even when I should run
Because you do not deserve my stability
I cannot move
Because I have no arms and legs
They have been swallowed
by the love inside me
Even when you toss me aside
I cannot become undone.
Even in a foreign land, I am still a rock
It is a burden all us rocks know too well.
Even when I want to break
I do not possess the ability
It's a disease you know
I think it might be hereditary.
In fact, I know it is.

- *Mummy and me*

I heard that you still weep for me
That the grief of my absence has buried you
Wailing at the moon for answers
They say that you have spent all of your money
on sweet yams and malt, anticipating my arrival
Have the neighbours stopped laughing yet?
Do you know that they think you've gone mad?
I often wondered how you could take such a risk
Trusting me to scatter your seeds
This trail of breadcrumbs has left me hungry
I am lost trying to find you.
Sometimes I see you in familiar strangers
hiding in European suits and office buildings
Sometimes I stay just a little longer in the sun,
wondering what you are feeling
Sometimes my heart aches that I cannot
phrase my love in a way that you can understand
se o ngbo mi, se o ngbo mi!
Can you hear me? Are you listening?
Your orphans are calling out. Away for too long.
The distance is more than plane flights and oceans
We are not home even when we are home
We speak many languages all in English
How cruel a fate
Birthed with two tongues that barely know each other
I silently scream from the diaspora
I wish you could hear us.

-   *M.I.A.*
Missing in Africa

For you I
Made my body a home
Built altars
Prayed on my knees
Begged for forgiveness
I wore many faces
Broke my back bending
Allowed my body to be
that needed bridge
From loneliness to peace
I created that pathway
You owe me.
Yet.
Nothing.

The perfect contortionist

How do I get over him?
How do I undo his work?
When his love has stained my skin
I reek.
Dependency has the strongest scent
I am consumed.
Swallowed whole by his feelings
I cannot take back my care
I cannot un-love him.

Therapy sessions

How are you?

Today I am angry.

I'm fine.

How are you?

I feel like I've been punched in the stomach
Gasping for air
No one can take the pain away
It cannot be shared
I must breathe through it
And in time it will pass
I know I'll be okay,
But it hurts.

I'm fine.

How are you?

I'm drowning under the weight of beautiful memories.

I'm fine.

How are you?

My heart is on fire.
Everyone run out
Run for cover
Before the flames consume you
There will be nothing left of you
My heart is on fire
Let me burn
Don't try and save it
My heart is on fire
Because of you.

I'm fine.

How are you?

I am okay
And not okay
At the same time
All the time

I'm fine.

The funny thing about anger is that
Once the dust has settled and
the hurricane has subsided
Your hollow reality is so obvious
Embarrassing almost
How much it has emptied your soul.

It is only anger that can feed you
and still leave you starving.

-   *Hunger*

In my mind
I've taken you back
Over and over again.
My regurgitating heart
Begs for you
To come home.

-   *A thousand heartbreaks*

I hate what your voice does
Suffocating me with old memories
Tying me up in familiarity
I cannot move
I want to scream
Watching my body
shamelessly cling to your words
Falling into forgotten smiles
Leftover laughs
I tried.
But I still do not hate you
I guess you cannot teach
an old heart new tricks.

-   *After he has left*

I compared my strengths
To your weaknesses
And wondered why I always came up short.

I must be many many women for you
I must be many many women for you
I must be strong but not intimidating
Soft but not weak
Loving but not needy
Loyal but not clingy
I must be many many women for you

I must be your mother and father
Both nurturer and protector
Best friend and lover
I must tiptoe around your heart
Being careful not to slip through a trap door
Before I get lost forever
You see I must be okay when you are closed
Silent, until you are ready to talk
Laying there.
Offering up my body as a sacrifice
Praying that you will feel man enough again
Bending around your needs
Listening to all the words you don't say
I must keep the doors of my heart open
Even when yours are shut
Just in case you need me

I must be many many women for you
I must swallow an hour glass for dinner and
Spit out perfect abs
Photoshop ready
Nudes by night, work dresses by day
Seductively modest
I must not wear too much makeup
Not like those girls, the ones your mother did not
like, the ones she warned you about
I must be many many women for you

I must be pure, untampered with.
As clean as they come, but still your dirty little secret
I must live up to standards that you will never have to
Because I must be accepting
I must get that you have a past, I must be forgiving
I must remember that I am over 25 and
it is too late to get picky
You see I must be many many women for you
And despite my mother's wishes
Chameleon is my new name
Constantly changing
So that your love for me can remain the same
You see I have been many many women

All hopelessly attempting to love you
And all the women in me are tired.
Tired of choking on I love yous
Knowing that each word is a prison sentence
in which you cannot afford the bail

So I cannot be many many women for you
I cannot pass down this schizophrenic love
I am accountable for my unborn daughters,
granddaughters, great granddaughters
I must teach them to never split into halves
Trying to make someone else feel whole
To never hold on to nothing
Just to tell others you have something
To be quick to recognise that if you
cannot be yourself, then this is not love.
The truth is there are many many women
Who have been many many women to many men
Who will do anything for a woman,
Apart from letting her be herself.

-        *Many, many women*

He stole my heart
And gave it back to me
When I begged him to keep it.

What do I do?
When you keep causing me pain
But I can't let go
Because I love you to death.

-    *Even when I don't want to*

Melodic moans, soft groans,
Whispers in the back ground
He says he likes the way our symphony sounds
So he tells me to be free
And just let my inhibitions take me
Away to ecstasy
Where no one will see, only his eyes
So he can find out where my passion lies
Release the desire lingering in my eyes
And fulfil the passion growing between my thighs
A gentle kiss, a soft squeeze
Is all it takes for me to be pleased
So now I believe that we're intertwined
More than physically
A sacred bond, man, woman, Adam, Eve
Running naked through the trees
Covering ourselves with love
In the form of leaves
But then I stop dreaming
Awaken.
To a man-made kind of love
Sweaty, artificial passion, diluted with sin
And who knew that dependency was an
aphrodisiac
Because *baby I need you*
Somehow translated into me trying to please you
Because each time he tells me that he loves me
I give in physically, spiritually, mentally
It's quite scary how easily my body
Gives in to our inability
To show real love.

Why can't I just have that simple love
Not tainted by
Rushed feelings
Heavy kisses
Sweaty sheets
Temporary highs
Awkward goodbyes
Sighs of relief.

- *Tired*

I still do not know love
But slave work
Working to be the perfect wife,
Back breaking, bending broad
Barely paid, acceptance whore
Beautiful zombie.
Live bodies, dead souls
Too late.
I opened my mouth, but had swallowed my voice
 But maybe if I became unconscious
Died in the eyes of the physical
Left you to your own misdemeanours
Found enough comfort in my pillows
And retired to my dreams
Then I can cast the first stone, right?
Because when I am awake I sin
Or do I sin because I am awake
Awake to psychological folk tales
That our ancestors poisoned us with
While sitting on the knee of love
Whispering hope of lies
That I can one day find comfort
With the reincarnation of my father
The only one to really love me,
right.
Ok, I believe you,
Are you happy now?
That I'm confused, emotionally bruised
Liberating my self-worth
Through lustful means
Telling you
 I'm the opened mind-closed legs kind of girl
Waiting for the 'one' in this loveless world
But the fire between my thighs
Clearly indicates my secret
I'm telling you no, so you kiss my neck

And my womanhood tells you liquid lies
That deceives me and you
That this is the only way to feel alive
Feel the blood rush through
As you toy with my conscience
Make me doubt my faith
That I'm less worthy to be at the pearly gates
That I don't deserve the husband
reserved for the virgin
maybe one or two is acceptable
But if I told you more
Would you back away,
 induce me into the mentality of a whore?
I don't care, remember.
But yet I still crave validation
Seeking resurrection
For my soul, having good reason to grow old
Holding on to the fact that there's more to life
Than what I see now
Can I deal the cards in this game please?
Because I need control over this vessel
That's slowly running dry
Losing all feeling, desperately hanging onto life
I'm going to be empty soon, die
Without a dignified legacy
There's got to be more to life,
Than life itself, right?
Because I'm losing this internal battle
Can't fight back because
I'm tied down by psychological shackles
Still trying to find my purpose
Indecision is my indecisive killer

So I'm dying, right?

-        *A short tour through a frustrated mind*

For too long I held you prisoner
Allowed my heart to become
handcuffs to your hands
I dreamt sweet amnesia filled dreams
that I forgot me
It took a dagger to the heart
Before I knew I was already bleeding
Standing over the edge with blind eyes
Playing a game of egos
I lost to love.

When I close my eyes
I see everything that I needed you to be.

-   *Sweet irony*

Then he took my left hand
And whispered forever in my ear
What was I to do?
How could I not believe him?

-   *Honey trap*

Every night I searched for us
in my memories.

-   *Insomnia*

I loved you so much that there was
nothing left for me.

And while we were sleeping
Our differences climbed into our love
And held us hostage
So I know you had no choice.

-        *Gunpoint*

Smiles behind tears
Tears behind smiles. For them.
They don't deserve
To see me, the real me
To have one over me
To pick at my soul
To eat at my heart
To suffocate my truth. No.
They don't deserve to see me
The real me
So I smile.

- *Deborah's song- part (i) Smile*

Look into my eyes
They are deceiving
Because tears inside are streaming
Like waterfalls
I fall
Yet I stand tall
And to all
My eyes deceive you.

- *Deborah's song – part (ii) deceiving eyes*

Sometimes I wish that you would cry
How else will your cleansing begin?
I beg you. Cry.
Cry for your fathers, brothers, sons
Cry for the tears you stored in your fists
Cry for every moment you silenced your voice
Cry for the mighty war that resides in your chest
Cry for the man that taught you
to shed blood before you do water
Cry because your heart has already started
Cry because your manhood will not betray you
Cry for all the times you didn't.
Cry because you need to
Cry like no one is watching
Just cry
Please cry
Not for me
But for you.

- *Masculinity*

I could see you
Every flaw
Every imperfection
I loved your broken pieces
The start of every masterpiece
You gave up too soon

I could see you. I wish you had believed me.

- *A beautiful mess*

It is terrifying
How wrong I was about them.
To see one ray of light
And confuse it for the sun.
To substitute my whole for only a piece.

I'm sorry for all the many nights
I've stumbled home
Looking for you at the bottom of an empty man.

-   *Dear future husband*

Still surprises me how we could
become oceans apart.

- *Distance*

My heart weeps for all the women
committing atrocities in the name of 'I love him'

You know it's time to leave
When you look inside yourself
And can only find him.

I fought for you
With every inch of my being
I let you run free
Through me
I gave you all I had
Because that's what you do for the one you love
I love you
I cannot let you leave
Even after you have left
I cannot let you leave
For you have stained every part of me
Your imprint is permanent
My mind constantly fights my heart for our memories
The thought of you leaves me aching for days
I miss you
I want to forget you
And not forget you
All at the same time
Why I am still fighting for you?

Do you know how much my heart aches for you?

The trouble with loving a broken person
Is that usually their selfishness allows them to hide
their cracked pieces
So much so that
They cannot just walk by
They must pursue you
You are just too good to let go
They cannot wait
They have not done the work
But they cannot miss out

What is the secret to your strength?
Does it hide in your locks?
Do you breathe flowers?
Does your skin taste like honey?

But what they do not know is that breaking you
and taking your pieces will not make them whole
And when they do realise this, and they
always eventually do
The pain is all too much for them
You are too much for them
Way too many complications
Now you are way too good
Too kind
Too forgiving
Too loving
But by then the damage has already been done
Well intentioned
They look at you like you should have always known
As if it is easy to take back the love they blindly stole

- *The lonely pedestal*

Do not punish me for loving
the version you showed me

-        *The breaking*

When he has left you
You will be tempted to answer stupid questions.
Like.
Was I good enough?
Was I pretty enough?
Too loud?
Too emotional?
Maybe if I said something sooner?
What if I just kept quiet?
Maybe I pushed too hard?
Maybe I didn't fight hard enough?

Trust me, do not do it
It will only leave you aching for days.

There are some nights…

I wish that I kept walking
Wish I'd never locked eyes with your soul
Never got lost in its abyss
Never tasted love
Never reached out my arms to save
Never knew you were drowning
Never forced to make that choice.
I wish it never had to be me or you
Did it have to be so final?
Why did I have to let go, surely there were
other ways to save you
Why did love betray me, forcing me to leave
knowing that my heart would stay

But then there are other nights…

I wish you would come back, standing by the door
Soaking wet from the rain, arms outstretched
Legs wide open, on your knees
Saying sorry with kisses
Knowing that I would forgive you
Healing with wine filled remedies
Nothing flowers can't fix
Filling our air with
I'm sorry, I love you, I will never do it again
Barricading ourselves in our union
No one in or out
Until we are suffocated by our beautiful moments
Dying. So that our love can once again live.

-        *Lovers torment*

When I think of you
I am split into oceans
Torn between
Loving every inch of your being
Or cursing the day you were born.

Do you know what it's like to have
your heart explode in your chest
and all you can do is smile
through your quivering lips?

\- *Every time they ask me where you are*

On my weakest days
They tell me *you're so strong*
I say
I'd rather be happy.

The love I have for you sits inside of me
And starves to death.
It didn't deserve that.

Because in my heart I said it was over
And I waved him away
But we left with kisses
That turns endings into wishes
Goodbyes into see-you-laters
Because what we said was fictitious
Unequally yoked but scared of loneliness…

I am tired. So very tired.
My heart is exhausted from hoping.
Watching myself everyday
continuing to love what
you once were.
Drawing from an empty well,
hoping for water.
Breaking. Every time.
Nothing inside.
But the saddest thing
is that I cannot stop. I have to look.
I have to try.
Just one more time.
I have to.

Sometimes I hate the fact that knowing
what I know I still want you so bad.

One of the hardest lessons that I was
forced to learn is that I love you is not
synonymous with I will stay
Someone can be madly in love with you
and still walk out the door.
Because will power is never enough,
for you cannot fight your way into a
feeling.
Your mind, body and soul
must be willing to do the work.

If you want to. Leave.
Do so.
Quickly.
Do not look back.
Give my heart a chance to forgive.
Be strong. Walk away.
You're not willing to do the work.
Accept that. Own it.
But you can't. So instead you wait. Linger. Beautiful
torment.
Like the scent of old musk, I'm not quite sure of your
exact departure.
Dangling a mirage of forevers.
Forcing my heart to push you out.
Doing your work.
Coward.

Sometimes it's not the breakup that kills you
It's the longing, the hoping,
the pulling and the tumbling
Down a road that has an inevitable end
Not sure if each day passes or approaches
Thinking that this is not so bad
Praying that our ending will be as beautiful as the sunset
But even she dies every night
Swallowed whole by the darkness

You see sometimes it's not the break up that kills you
It's the longing, the hoping,
the pulling and the tumbling
It's all the days that come before
Choking on old memories,
knowing that we will never work
Understanding that *I'll love you forever* also has an end

Sometimes it's not the break up that kills you
It's the longing, the hoping,
the pulling and the tumbling
It's the loving, then the fighting,
then the loving, then the fighting
Tired. We stop trying
Then it's the awkward silences
All the words we didn't mean
The distance that grows in between
It's the distinct aftertaste of routine.

Sometimes it's not the break up that kills you
It's the longing, the hoping,
the pulling and the tumbling
So worn out,
What we had died long before we ended.
You see sometimes it's not the break up
that kills you.

DAWN

That moment when you can see the sunrise, when you can breathe again. You can finally feel the blood rush through, the sound of your heartbeat is now a tender reminder that you have so many wonderful reasons to be alive. You thank the universe for her mercy, because all of those reasons start and end with you. You have accepted your journey, thanked her for the pain, the lessons, the things you had to go through. At the crack of dawn, you can see the light shine on your scars, see them for what they are, absolutely breath-taking, because each one tells a story. Your story, of how you lived through wars and came out beautiful. In this light you can see what others could see for so long; that you are made of magic.

DAWN

How to get over a break up...

1. Cry and cry some more
   (you are not weak when you break into oceans)
2. Do not isolate yourself.
   God made shoulders to be leant on
3. Go out. Adorn your body with jewels.
   Wear that dress. Dance. Dance until you sweat.
   Dance until you forget that some men
   have no business playing with hearts
4. Be wary of hungry little boys
   (broken hearts smell like easy sex and no
   commitment)
5. Only when you are ready, delete/burn/throw away old
   pictures, letters, jumpers etc. This part will require
   courage. It will feel like someone is ripping
   your soul from your chest, but you are stronger
   than you think
6. Redecorate your room
7. Try a new hairstyle
8. Go to the gym
9. Write a list of all the things that make you happy
10. Do them.

There is a day that is coming
When I will be over you
Memories of you will no longer
choke me mid-sentence
It will no longer break me
when I tell others of our fate
My nights will no longer end in tears
You will feel the urge to call me
When her love does not satisfy
When her hands cannot
commit to your needs
You will search through every part of her
but you will not find me
Each night you will drink at her well
hoping for honey but only tasting salt
By dawn your mind will yearn for me
By dusk your body will scream my name
She will break each time
she tastes my lips on your skin
You will want to call me
because you miss me
My absence has become unbearable
You will finally realise that the oceans and
mountains separate us.
There is no map left for you
For I am no longer waiting for you
to find me
I have left
Taken my shattered pieces
and built a home
You will call me
Say that you finally understand
That this was something you had to go through
I will answer but my heart
will no longer be listening
I will make space for another to love me

And I will love them harder than ever before
A love well earned
A welcome home gift for battling
their way through
to my dying heart.

- *One day*

For those who think that I am strong
I am not strong because I wanted to be
I became strong by default.
With every let down
Every disappointment
Every tear that fell
For I fought not for sport
But for survival.

I'm tired of writing this sad song.
Wallowing is not for me.
Yes, I need to heal.
But this is a journey of self-growth, self-discovery
It's time. To be happy.
Demand back my joy.
I do not possess the power to change. Change.
True change is organic and genuine.
Take off your shackles young one
Unload this weight
Come inside where it is warm
Kick off your shoes. Rest.
As I said I'm tired of writing this sad song.
My new melody awaits…

I want to be that woman
Whose words drip of sweet honey
Full of grace
And seasoned with salt.

-    *Col 4:6*

A lot of heartache would be avoided
if we were honest about our weaknesses.

-   *Transparent*

Acceptance should never be an excuse
for bad behaviour.
Repeat after me
Today I will try to be better…

Love is not insecure, selfish or blind
It keeps no records of wrongs,
as it is patient and kind
Love will not make a fool out of you.

- *Daily reminders*

Forgive yourself for every time you said *No*
Every time you created boundaries
Stood up for what you believed in
Walked away from what no longer gave you peace
Said that you wanted more
Chose to be protective over your space
For your time to be just that. Yours.

It is okay.
Even when the choice is just out of two.

It is okay to choose you.

That moment when you finally become the
love of your life.

Seize that moment
Revel in that moment
Don't ever let it go.

-   *Self-love*

You have one role as a parent and that is
to be there, mentally and physically.
You may not have all
the right things to say
You will get it wrong at times
But that is okay
So do not run
Do not give up
Because as long as there are
two heartbeats and one roof
Your job is safe

Just be there. Breathing. Waiting for me.

\-   *Employee of the month, my mother*

When we find ourselves constantly fault-finding
Remember
It's a lot easier to look down on others
when we are standing on our egos.

- *Checkpoint*

If only you knew how magical you truly are…

I used to be so angry
Filled with rage
My pain was so obvious it embarrassed me.
Days I would wake up with my head on fire.
I wondered if the aching would ever stop.
Until time came with her healing hands
Ushering me into each day with love.
I know. When your heart is broken it is difficult to
feel anything else.
But believe me when I say it gets easier.
You will smile again.
You will smile again.
You will love harder than you ever did before.
You will survive this.
You are going to be okay.
In fact, even better than okay.
You are going to be good. Happy.
Do not be angry at the universe.
Thank her for the growth
Forgive yourself.
Forgive them.
Open yourself up to the healing.
And get on with the rest of your life.

I thought I wanted someone just like me.
And he was just like me.
A broken me.
A scared me.
A former me.

When I speak of you
Your name will be followed by gratitude.
Thankful for our memories
Thankful for the lessons
Thankful for the growth
Because when I lost you I was forced to find myself
So I'll leave now
And with time I will be okay with this
But remember me
Remember I saw the most beautiful part of you
The light in you
It's in you
So remember me, when you can't seem to find the light.

Repeat after me
*Sometimes I will get it wrong but it's never ever
okay not to try*

-    *Beauty in mistakes*

You are and always will be
enough.

-    *Things my mother taught me*

To everyone I ignored.
My deepest apologies
I wanted to run
So far
I couldn't risk you seeing
How empty
I was becoming.

Sometimes when your world turns upside down
It's God's way of forcing you to do what you want to do.
What you need to do. And not just what's easiest.

-      *Unusual miracles*

I love you.
Yes, you.
Even when you're stupid
enough to believe
you're no good, not needed.
When you're too loud.
Too much
Too quiet
Too moody
Too defensive
Too fat
Too skinny
Too dark
Too light

I love you.

- *A note to self*

Don't call me pretty or beautiful
Don't fall in love with the arch of my back or the
fullness of my lips
For I cannot be held responsible for such distractions
Call me hard work
Call me complicated
Call me art
Because that way when you stay
I can believe it's for all the right reasons
It's far too much effort being 'pretty' for you.

Sometimes letting go can turn
painful endings into beautiful beginnings.

Pressed against my chest
Watching, as his eyes cautiously travel down
Point to where it hurts
Tears in my eyes, holding my left breast
He places his hand over mine
Let me kiss it better.

-    *When love returns and love knows you've been through*
                     enough already

Scars are nothing but
triumphant reminders
that we can be healed
from our open wounds.
It's usually the ugliest scars
that tell the most
beautiful stories.

In a world full of opinions
Let my walk be your witness
In a world full of rebuttals
Let my walk be your witness
In a world where everyone is fighting
To have their voice heard
Let my walk be your witness

My mind is a mess
Let my walk be your witness
My mind is hurting
Let my walk be your witness
My mind begs for clarity
Let my walk be your witness

When I need to be strong
Let my walk be your witness
When I need to be brave
Let my walk be your witness
When I need to be kind
Let my walk be your witness

Let my walk be your witness
Let your love be my witness.

- *Walk*

Handing over the task of loving yourself is
handing over your superpower.

- *Risky business*

She is a verb in a world full of nouns.

- *A poem for my sister*

When I was younger I wanted to
change the world.
As I got older the thought alone
made me shiver
The world looked too dark
Too cold
Too grim
Way too much of a task for just one
Until I finally realised that every time
I shone
My little light into the darkness
I was changing the world
Bit by bit
Loving in poems
Breathing in ink
One beautiful word at a time.

There is a force that is so much deeper than I
Wiser than I
Larger than I.

-    *Love*

When my mind was full with so many
painful questions,
You came and filled it with flowers
Short ones
Long ones
Colourful ones
Dark ones
Thorny ones.

-    *The power of poetry*

Sometimes it's the small ones that do it
When nothing else seems to explain
some of the longest nights
It's all the words that aren't said
That speak volumes
Sometimes it's the small ones.

-   *Short poems*

To the yellow
Spanish town
Big bellied
Jamaican man
Who found my smile
At the bottom of the 149 bus
On valentine's day.
Holding flowers, he forgot weren't for me.
Your words kissed me like poetry

Aye gyal yuh too sweet, spend some time wid me
suh some ah you sweetness rub off pon mi.

Thank you. I needed that.

Real eyes, realise, real lies
Or is it real eyes, tell real lies
That causes us to recognise the reality of our demise
But I don't know the answer
All I know is
These complex tools, that we call eyes
Sometimes get me into trouble
I have to be careful
Not too stare to hard
At these girls
Before I give the so-called
'I think I'm all that, take your man in a second'
kind of look
But if you looked
You would realise
That I am all that and your man
would want me in a second
Just because of my look and
If you could look past
What your peripheral vision
Allows you to see
You would have realised
That it was a look of human affection
And not the bogus views of modern society
But I guess it's the silence in eyes
That screams the loudest songs
Because with a simple wink
I can give you the...
'I think you're kinda nice' kind of look

I'm going to slow down my pace and
allow you to cross the road, kind of look
And if you approach me right
I might tell you my real name, age and number
kind of look
But it's just a look

Because in the blink of an eye
These eyes can become the deadliest weapon
That would shock the masses at the
level of destruction possible
If only you knew
I'd probably get calls from Stalin,
Asking me to come kick it
With George B, Osama and the disciples of Mussolini
But eyes are not about politics
Eyes are the windows of the soul
A recollection comprising of memories, sensations,
feelings, emotions
Like the look of a new born, flowers or oceans
The only place where the truth can't hide
Because it's the cornea, optic nerve, iris and retina
That it chooses to reside, confide
Within a scientific truth
That exposes us
When our mouths choose the path of lies

But did you know that they are
the most complex organs you possess
Other than your brain?
So by my calculations
The abuse they receive is criminally insane
But if we knew that every single hour they process over
36,000 pieces of information
Then maybe the way we look at the world may no longer
remain the same
36,000 ways to say I love you
36,000 ways to appreciate a sunset
36,000 ways to have your heart broken
From one look
Seeing him in the arms of another girl
Rather go blind
Then see him happy not in your world

But in another hour you'll remember
His 36,000 smiles
And realise upon each glance
How you fell deeper within his beauty
36,000 times you nearly got caught slipping
Staring at him while he's sleeping
Frightened that he'll wake up
And you'll give him the…
'I'm sprung, helplessly in love and
wouldn't change a thing' kind of look

Because as hard as they try
My eyes just cannot lie
So I guess they never rest
They say over a normal life span
That is minus, STDs, knife and gun crime
We take in over 24 million images
So appreciate them.
Because life is way too short.

- A poem about eyes

Black women learnt to love themselves.
Until they were full.
Until they did not need yours.
Until they realised that their own was enough.

-   *Full*

I put so much pressure on myself
Trying to write something good for them
That I was never good enough
Before I could even conceive the words
I wondered would they like her?
Will they accept her?
Until I started to write something good for me.
Then I was free
So never ever give into the pressure
Because if they like it. Good.
And if they do not. That is okay.
For it was not written for them anyway.

- *To every artist*

I deserve to be wanted
I do not have to convince anyone to do the work
I have faith in love
I believe in her power
And if he no longer does. I have learnt.
That is okay
Because I want a love that knows no barriers
That will climb mountains and cross seas
Someone who sees our love
as an ocean worth drowning in
Where egos come to die
Someone who can stare confrontation in the face.
And stand.
Someone who sees the darkest parts of me as the
most important reason to stay
Someone who is willing to fight
Someone who understands that hearts are fragile
and should be handled with care.
Someone who believes that our fairytale
is not fiction just untold.
Someone who will nurture the light in me.
Someone who comprehends that support works
both ways.
Someone that practices consistency.
Someone that will recite these words back to me
when I am settling for less.
Someone who will not leave me.
Someone who is patient enough to commit
to the journey.
That's the love I deserve.

Never ever be afraid to start again.

You see all that pain you're feeling?
Yeah.
That too is also temporary.

And on a rare day, when I find myself about to cry
I inhale
Exhale
And
Allow your memory to wash over me
Because like the tide,
This too shall pass.

\-   *Joy comes in the AM*

I am too much
Too much woman
Too much black
Too much black woman

I am a man eater
Too much men swallowed whole
Too much failed conquests

I am Eve
Too much of the original
Too much creator
Too much life
Too much storm
Too much rain

I am a tsunami
Too much opinion
Too much voice
Too much noise

I am my ancestors' oppressor's sexiest nightmare
Too much body
Too much curve
Too much sin
Too much freedom
Too much black
Too much black freedom

I am too many ugly black girls
Too much tears
Too much careless words
Too much let downs
Too much pain

I am back bone
Too much fight
Too much sweat
Too much blood
Too much love
Too many hours of labour

I am my mother's words
Too much beauty
Too much passion
Too much fire

I am too much of what I have been through
Too much woman
Too much black
Too much black woman
So it is okay,
if I am too much for you to handle.

-   *I am*

Self-love takes **practice**.

1. Remember that you do not know it all
2. Accept that you may not always have the answer
3. Write a list of all the things that make you happy, then do them
4. Look your fears dead in the face
5. Smile at strangers
6. Laugh a little louder
7. Hug a few seconds longer, tighter.
8. Say please and thank you
9. Hold the door open
10. Be on time
11. Stand up against bullies
12. Never tolerate injustice
13. Fight for what you believe in
14. Never forget to give some of that love (that you so freely give to others) back to yourself
15. Feed the homeless
16. Listen more
17. Deliver your honesty with kind words
18. Be more generous
19. Catch up with your friends
20. Stay out an extra hour
21. Dance till your legs ache
22. Remember it is okay to cry. You are not weak when you cry
23. Let your word be your bond
24. Travel the world
25. Eat things that you've never tried before. Taste a different culture.
26. Exercise more
27. Be your own cheerleader
28. Have faith
29. If you love them. Tell them.
30. Be all in, never half-hearted.
31. Give compliments

32. Swallow your pride.
(I promise you won't put on a single pound)
33. Apologise when you've done something wrong
34. Accept when you have hurt someone's feelings
35. Don't give up on your dreams. Even when you think you look stupid, never give up.
36. Always check your motives. Ask yourself: why?
37. Let love drive you
38. Always try
39. Remember you are much stronger than you think

I know that I cannot change some of the things that
happened between us or the way it happened.
But can you do me this one favour?
Can you forgive me?
Can you bring down the walls I forced you to build?
I desperately want to start again.
A fresh start can only begin with you.
I need you to know that I am trying.
Trying to find my way back to you.
The truth is I was scared.
I allowed you to become a stranger to me.
But I want something substantial with you and most
of all I want to do things God's way.
I spent too long disappointed and hurt,
that I made decisions based on
feelings and not faith.
I took it out on you.
That was wrong.
I am still glad I met you, you're always going to be
the one for me.
I just wish I could have done things differently,
allowed you to see me properly without the added
distractions.
I cannot change the way things have turned out,
but I would like to start again
(only if you want to of course)
So hi Sarah, my name is Sarah
And I love you
I will never leave you
Never again will I replace you with another

-    *When you finally find your way back home*

about the author

Sarah Aluko is a poet and writer, born and raised in London by West African parents. At the age of 15, she wrote her first poem which was published on an online poetry magazine. Heavily influenced by the likes of Maya Angelou and John Agard, Sarah knew that expressing herself in poems was not something she could ignore. However, despite her longing to write, she went on to complete her law degree and pursue a career in finance. Through one of the most difficult periods of her life she was able reflect and pour herself into her words. Writing became her solitude, her safe haven. After travelling to many different countries around the world and writing away her fears, Sarah finally was able to give birth to this collection, her firstborn.

Taking you on a journey of self-discovery and healing, the book tackles themes such as love, loss, femininity, heartbreak and survival. Through her poems she gives a raw, honest account of her journey through womanhood, showing us that she, like so many others, is not a one dimensional creature: she has many different layers and her own unique story to tell. Sarah aims to show readers that it is important to embrace every part of yourself, including parts that we consider to be dark and ugly, as this is the only way to truly survive in a world that is constantly telling you what version of yourself you are should be.

about the book

Firstborn is a collection of poetry. The book is divided into three sections Dusk, Twilight and Dawn. Each section unveils a different mountain, deals with a different heartache and conquers a different war. The book depicts a journey of redemption through self-discovery. The common themes running throughout the book are love, femininity, abuse, survival and heartbreak. Firstborn is a story about a young woman writing her way back to herself.

about the illustrator

East London based artist Lola Betiku draws inspiration from various aspects of life including literature, music, pop culture and religion but more recently her African heritage versus her British upbringing. Through different expressions of art, be it abstract, digital or portraiture, she enjoys exploring ideas and interpretations of identity to evoke emotion.

"it's all work in progress!... for me art is refuge for the eyes and mind to be free in creativity through imagination and wonder. I view each piece of work as a continuous journey where internal progress is guaranteed no matter what the external standards of the world may be. The rhythm of each line, the colours, strokes and textures coming together on any given canvas can reveal a variation of stories which to me is the beauty of art - it's not finished even after the paintbrush is put down!"

L. Betiku

For more information, please visit www.labetmakesart.co.uk

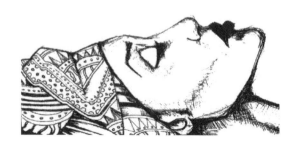